Babyt

outside

Brown Watson

ENGLAND

swing

moon

flowers

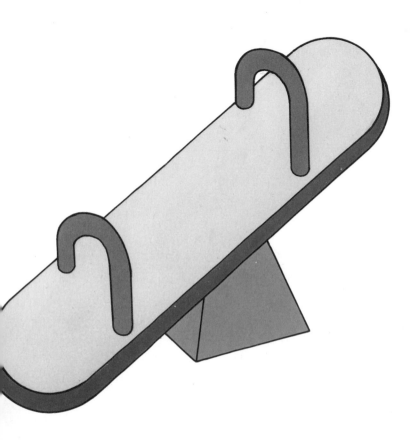

see-saw

plane

car

stars

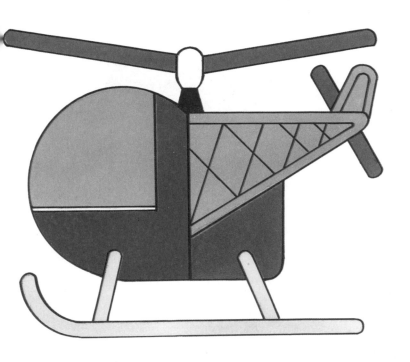

helicopter

slide

tractor

sun

umbrella

truck

crane

watering can

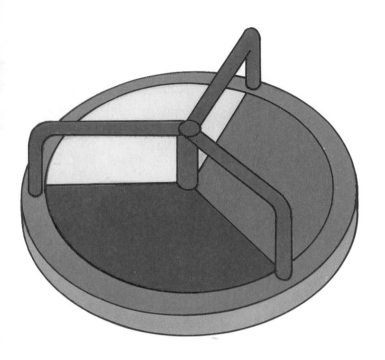

roundabout

house

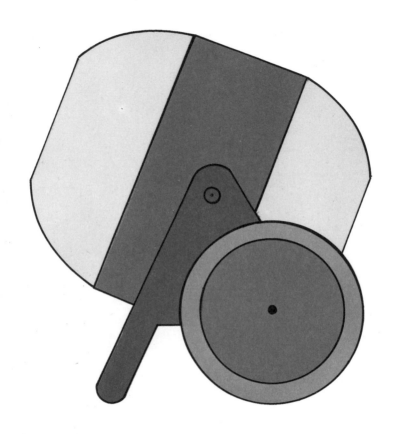

cement mixer

bus

dog

climbing frame

bird

bicycle

church

ambulance

cat

butterfly